THE WOMEN AND THE

Also by Nikki Giovanni

Black Feeling, Black Talk / Black Judgement
Re:Creation
Spin a Soft Black Song
Gemini
A Dialogue: James Baldwin and Nikki Giovanni
My House
A Poetic Equation: Conversations between
    Nikki Giovanni and Margaret Walker
Ego Tripping and Other Poems for Young Readers

THE WOMEN AND THE MEN

by Nikki Giovanni

WILLIAM MORROW AND COMPANY, INC.
NEW YORK   1975

FIRST MORROW QUILL PAPERBACK EDITION

Library of Congress Cataloging-in-Publication Data

Giovanni, Nikki
    The women and the men.

    Poems.
    I. Title.
PS3557.I55W6   1975   811'.5'4   75-16237
ISBN 0-688-07947-4

Design by H. Roberts

Printed in the United States of America

18   19   20

For Tommy and Stacie
the future men and women

CONTENTS

III.   AND SOME PLACES

I. The Women

THE WOMEN GATHER
(for Joe Strickland)

the women gather
because it is not unusual
to seek comfort in our hours of stress
    a man must be buried

it is not unusual
that the old bury the young
    though it is an abomination

it is not strange
that the unwise and the ungentle
carry the banner of humaneness
    though it is a castration of the spirit

it no longer shatters the intellect
that those who make war
call themselves diplomats

we are no longer surprised
that the unfaithful pray loudest
every sunday in every church
and sometimes in rooms facing east
    though it is a sin and a shame

    so how do we judge a man

most of us love from our need to love not
because we find someone deserving

most of us forgive because we have trespassed not
because we are magnanimous

most of us comfort because we need comforting
our ancient rituals demand that we give
what we hope to receive

    and how do we judge a man

we learn to greet when meeting
to cry when parting
and to soften our words at times of stress

the women gather
with cloth and ointment
their busy hands bowing to laws that decree
willows shall stand swaying but unbroken
against even the determined wind of death

    we judge a man by his dreams
not alone his deeds
    we judge a man by his intent
not alone his shortcomings
    we judge a man because it is not unusual
to know him through those who love him

the women gather strangers
to each other because
they have loved a man

it is not unusual to sift
through ashes
and find an unburnt picture

ALL I GOTTA DO

all i gotta do
is sit and wait
sit and wait
and it's gonna find
me
all i gotta do
is sit and wait
if i can learn
how

what i need to do
is sit and wait
cause i'm a woman
sit and wait
what i gotta do
is sit and wait
cause i'm a woman
it'll find me

you get yours
and i'll get mine
if i learn
to sit and wait
you got yours
i want mine
and i'm gonna get it
cause i gotta get it
cause i need to get it
if i learn how

thought about calling
for it on the phone
asked for a delivery
but they didn't have it

thought about going
to the store to get it
walked to the corner
but they didn't have it

called your name
in my sleep
sitting and waiting
thought you would awake me
called your name
lying in my bed
but you didn't have it
offered to go get it
but you didn't have it
so i'm sitting

all i know
is sitting and waiting
waiting and sitting
cause i'm a woman
all i know
is sitting and waiting
cause i gotta wait
wait for it to find
me

ONCE A LADY TOLD ME

like my mother and her grandmother before
i paddle around the house
in soft-soled shoes
chasing ghosts from corners
with incense
they are such a disturbance my ghosts
they break my bric-a-brac and make
me forget to turn my heating stove

the children say you must come to live
with us   all my life i told them i've lived
with you   now i shall live with myself

the grandchildren say it's disgraceful
you in this dark house with the curtains
pulled   snuff dripping from your chin
would they be happier if i smoked   cigarettes

i was very exquisite once   very small and well courted
some would say a beauty when my hair was plaited
and i was bustled up

my children wanted my life
and now they want my death

but i shall pad around my house
in my purple soft-soled shoes
i'm very happy now
it's not so very neat, you know, but it's my
life

EACH SUNDAY

if she wore her dresses
the same length as mine
people would gossip viciously
about her morals

if i slept   head barely touching
the string of freshwater fake pearls
mouth slightly open   eyebrows knitted
almost into a frown
people would accuse me of running around
too much

suddenly her eyes springing away
from her sleep intensely
scope the pulpit and fall
on me

i wonder did she dream
while baking cold-water cornbread
of being a great reporter churning
all the facts together and creating
the truth
did she think   while patching the torn pants
and mending the socks of her men   of standing
arms outstretched before a great world
body offering her solution for peace
what did she feel wringing the neck
of Sunday's chicken breaking the beans
of her stifled life

she sits each sunday black
dress falling below her knees which have drifted
apart defining a void
in the temple of her life in the church of her god
strong and staunch and hopeful
that we never change
places

POEM FOR FLORA

when she was little
and colored and ugly with short
straightened hair
and a very pretty smile
she went to sunday school to hear
'bout nebuchadnezzar the king
of the jews

and she would listen

shadrach, meshach and abednego in the fire

and she would learn

how god was neither north
nor south east or west
with no color but all
she remembered was that
Sheba was Black and comely

and she would think

i want to be
like that

THE DECEMBER OF MY SPRINGS

in the december of my springs
i long for the days
i shall somehow have
free from children and dinners
and people i have grown stale with

this time i think i'll face love
with my heart instead of my glands
rather than hands clutching to satiate
my fingers will stroke to satisfy
i think it might be good
to decide rather than to need

that pitter-patter rhythm of rain
sliding on city streets is as satisfying
to me as this quiet has become
and like the raindrop i accede to my nature

perhaps there will be no
difference between the foolishness of age
and the foolishness of youth
some say we are responsible
for those we love
others know we are responsible
for those who love us

so i sit waiting
for a fresh thought
to stir the atmosphere

i'm glad i'm not iron
else i would be burned
by now

THE LIFE I LED

i know my upper arms will grow
flabby it's true
of all the women in my family

i know that the purple veins
like dead fish in the Seine
will dot my legs one day
and my hands will wither while
my hair turns grayish white   i know that
one day my teeth will move when
my lips smile
and a flutter of hair will appear
below my nose   i hope
my skin doesn't change to those blotchy
colors

i want my menses to be undifficult
i'd very much prefer staying firm and slim
to grow old like a vintage wine fermenting
in old wooden vats with style
i'd like to be exquisite   i think

i will look forward to grandchildren
and my flowers   all my knickknacks in their places
and that quiet of the bombs not falling in cambodia
settling over my sagging breasts

i hope my shoulder finds a head that needs nestling
and my feet find a footstool after a good soaking
with epsom salts

i hope i die
warmed
by the life that i tried
to live

REVOLUTIONARY DREAMS

i used to dream militant
dreams of taking
over america to show
these white folks how it should be
done
i used to dream radical dreams
of blowing everyone away with my perceptive powers
of correct analysis
i even used to think i'd be the one
to stop the riot and negotiate the peace
then i awoke and dug
that if i dreamed natural
dreams of being a natural
woman doing what a woman
does when she's natural
i would have a revolution

THE GENIE IN THE JAR

(*for Nina Simone*)

take a note and spin it around spin it around don't
prick your finger
take a note and spin it around
on the Black loom on the Black loom
careful baby
don't prick your finger

take the air and weave the sky
around the Black loom around the Black loom
make the sky sing a Black song sing a blue song
sing my song make the sky sing a Black song
from the Black loom from the Black loom
careful baby
don't prick your finger

take a genie and put her in a jar
put her in a jar
wrap the sky around her
take the genie and put her in a jar
wrap the sky around her
listen to her sing
sing a Black song our Black song
from the Black loom
singing to me
from the Black loom
careful baby
don't prick your finger

POEM FOR ARETHA

cause nobody deals with aretha—a mother with four
    children—having to hit the road
they always say "after she comes
home" but nobody ever says what it's like
to get on a plane for a three-week tour
the elation of the first couple of audiences the good
feeling of exchange the running on the high
you get from singing good
and loud and long telling the world
what's on your mind

then comes the eighth show on the sixth day the
    beginning
to smell like the plane or bus the if-you-forget-your
    toothbrush
in-one-spot-you-can't-brush-until-the-second-show the
    strangers
pulling at you cause they love you but you having no love
to give back
the singing the same songs night after night day after day
and if you read the gossip columns the rumors that your
    husband
is only after your fame
the wondering if your children will be glad to see you and
    maybe
the not caring if they are the scheming to get out
of just one show and go just one place where some
    doe-doe-dupaduke
won't say "just sing one song, please"

nobody mentions how it feels to become a freak
because you have talent and how
no one gives a damn how you feel
but only cares that aretha franklin is here like maybe
that'll stop:

chickens from frying
eggs from being laid
crackers from hating
and if you say you're lonely or scared or tired how they
    always
just say "oh come off it" or "did you see
how they loved you did you see huh did you?"
which most likely has nothing to do with you anyway
and i'm not saying aretha shouldn't have talent and i'm
    certainly
not saying she should quit
singing but as much as i love her i'd vote "yes" to her
doing four concerts a year and staying home or doing
    whatever
she wants and making records cause it's a shame
the way we are killing her
we eat up artists like there's going to be a famine at the
    end
of those three minutes when there are in fact an
    abundance
of talents just waiting let's put some
of the giants away for a while and deal with them like
    they have
a life to lead

aretha doesn't have to relive billie holiday's life doesn't
    have
to relive dinah washington's death but who will
stop the pattern

she's more important than her music—if they must be
    separated—
and they should be separated when she has to pass out
    before
anyone recognizes she needs
a rest and i say i need
aretha's music

she is undoubtedly the one person who put everyone on
notice
she revived johnny ace and remembered lil green aretha
        sings
"i say a little prayer" and dionne doesn't
want to hear it anymore
aretha sings "money won't change you"
but james can't sing "respect" the advent
of aretha pulled ray charles from marlboro country
and back into
the blues made nancy wilson
try one more time forced
dionne to make a choice (she opted for the movies)
and diana ross had to get an afro wig pushed every
Black singer into Blackness and negro entertainers
into negroness you couldn't jive
when she said "you make me/feel" the blazers
had to reply "gotta let a man be/a man"
aretha said "when my show was in the lost and found/you
        came
along to claim it" and joplin said "maybe"
there has been no musician whom her very presence
        hasn't
affected whem humphrey wanted her to campaign
        she said
"woeman's only hueman"
and he pressured james brown
they removed otis cause the combination was too strong
the impressions had to say "lord have mercy/we're
        moving
on up"
the Black songs started coming from the singers on stage
        and the dancers

in the streets
aretha was the riot was the leader if she had said "come
let's do it" it would have been done
temptations say why don't we think about it
                    think about it
                    think about it

AND SOMETIMES I SIT

and sometimes i sit
down at my typewriter
and i think
not of someone
cause there isn't anyone
to think
about and i wonder
is it worth it

FOR A LADY OF PLEASURE NOW RETIRED

some small island birthed
her and a big (probably) white ship took her
from mother to come
to america's recreation

she lives in the top of my building
i only know her through her eyes
she is old now not only from years
but from aging

one gets the impression she was most
beautiful and like good wine
or a semiprecious jewel touted out
for the pleasure of those
who could afford
her recreation

her head is always high
though the set of her mouth shows
it's not easy
she asks nothing
seems to have something
to give but no one to give it
to if ever she gave it
to anyone

age requires happy memories like louvenia smiled
when she died and though her doctor had told her not
to there was pork cooking
on the stove
there are so many new mistakes
for a lady of pleasure

that can be made it shouldn't be
necessary to repeat the old
ones

and it was cold
on the elevator that morning
when i spoke to her and foolishly asked
        how are you
she smiled and tilted her head
        at least, i said, the sun is
        shining
and her eyes smiled   yes
and i was glad to be
there to say through spirits
        there is a new creation
to her

POEM FOR A LADY
WHOSE VOICE I LIKE

so he said: you ain't got no talent
    if you didn't have a face
    you wouldn't be nobody

and she said: god created heaven and earth
    and all that's Black within them

so he said: you ain't really no hot stuff
    they tell me plenty sisters
    take care better business than you

and she said: on the third day he made chitterlings
    and all good things to eat
    and said: "that's good"

so he said: if the white folks hadn't been under
    yo skirt and been giving you the big play
    you'd a had to come on uptown like everybody else

and she replied: then he took a big Black greasy rib
    from adam and said we will call this woeman and her
    name will be sapphire and she will divide into four
    parts
that simone may sing a song

and he said: you pretty full of yourself ain't chu

so she replied: show me someone not full of herself
    and i'll show you a hungry person

EGO TRIPPING
(*there may be a reason why*)

i was born in the congo
I walked to the fertile crescent and built
      the sphinx
I designed a pyramid so tough that a star
      that only glows every one hundred years falls
      into the center giving divine perfect light
I am bad

I sat on the throne
      drinking nectar with allah
I got hot and sent an ice age to europe
      to cool my thirst
My oldest daughter is nefertiti
      the tears from my birth pains
      created the nile
I am a beautiful woman

I gazed on the forest and burned
      out the sahara desert
      with a packet of goat's meat
      and a change of clothes
I crossed it in two hours
I am a gazelle so swift
      so swift you can't catch me

      For a birthday present when he was three
I gave my son hannibal an elephant
      He gave me rome for mother's day
My strength flows ever on

My son noah built new/ark and
I stood proudly at the helm
      as we sailed on a soft summer day
I turned myself into myself and was
      jesus

men intone my loving name
All praises All praises
I am the one who would save

I sowed diamonds in my back yard
My bowels deliver uranium
    the filings from my fingernails are
    semi-precious jewels
    On a trip north
I caught a cold and blew
My nose giving oil to the arab world
I am so hip even my errors are correct
I sailed west to reach east and had to round off
    the earth as I went
    The hair from my head thinned and gold was laid
    across three continents

I am so perfect so divine so ethereal so surreal
I cannot be comprehended
    except by my permission

I mean . . . I . . . can fly
    like a bird in the sky . . .

HOUSECLEANING

i always liked housecleaning
even as a child
i dug straightening
the cabinets
putting new paper on
the shelves
washing the refrigerator
inside out
and unfortunately this habit has
carried over and i find
i must remove you
from my life

EVER WANT TO CRAWL

ever want to crawl
in someone's arms
white out the world
in someone's arms
and feel the world
of someone's arms
it's so hot in hell
if i don't sweat
i'll melt

MOTHER'S HABITS

i have all
my mother's habits
i awake in the middle of night
to smoke a cigarette
i have a terrible fear of flying
and i don't like being alone
in the dark
sleep is a sport we all
participate in
it's the scourge of youth
and a necessity of old age
though it only hastens the day
when dissolution is inevitable
i grow tired
like my mother doing without
even one small word
that says i care
and like my mother i shall fade
into my dreams
no longer caring
either

II. The Men

THE WAY I FEEL

i've noticed i'm happier
when i make love
with you
and have enough left
over to smile at my doorman

i've realized i'm fulfilled
like a big fat cow
who has just picked
for a carnation contentment
when you kiss your special place
right behind my knee

i'm as glad as mortar
on a brick that knows
another brick is coming
when you walk through
my door

most time when you're around
i feel like a note
roberta flack is going to sing

in my mind you're a clock
and i'm the second hand sweeping
around you sixty times an hour
twenty-four hours a day
three hundred sixty-five days a year
and an extra day
in leap year
cause that's the way
that's the way
that's the way i feel
about you

KIDNAP POEM

ever been kidnapped
by a poet
if i were a poet
i'd kidnap you
put you in my phrases and meter
you to jones beach
or maybe coney island
or maybe just to my house
lyric you in lilacs
dash you in the rain
blend into the beach
to complement my see
play the lyre for you
ode you with my love song
anything to win you
wrap you in the red Black green
show you off to mama
yeah if i were a poet i'd kid
nap you

COMMUNICATION

if music is the most universal language
just think of me as one whole note

if science has the most perfect language
picture me as MC^2

since mathematics can speak to the infinite
imagine me as 1 to the first power

what i mean is   one day
i'm gonna grab your love
and you'll be
satisfied

I WANT TO SING

i want to sing
a piercing note
lazily throwing my legs
across the moon
my voice carrying all the way
over to your pillow
    i want you

i need i swear to loll
about the sun
and have it smelt me
the ionosphere carrying
my ashes all
the way over
to your pillow
    i want you

LUXURY

i suppose living
in a materialistic society
luxury
to some would be having
more than what you need

living in an electronic age seeing
the whole world by pushing a button
the *nth* degree might perhaps be
adequately represented by having
someone there to push
the buttons for you

i have thought if only
i could become rich and famous i would
live luxuriously in new york knowing
famous people eating
in expensive restaurants calling
long distance anytime i want

but you held me
one evening and now i know
the ultimate luxury
of your love

POEM

like a will-o'-the-wisp in the night
on a honeysuckle breeze
a moment sticks
us together

like a dolphin being
tickled on her stomach
my sea of love flip-flops all
over my face

like the wind blowing
across a field of wheat
your smile whispers to my inner ear

with the relief of recognition
i bend to your eyes
casually
raping me

AUTUMN POEMS

the heat
you left with me
last night
still smolders
the wind catches
your scent
and refreshes
my senses

i am a leaf
falling from your tree
upon which i was
impaled

HAMPTON, VIRGINIA

the birds flew south
earlier this year
and flowers wilted under the glare
of frost
nature puts her house in order

the weather reports say this
will be the coldest winter
already the perch have burrowed
deep into the lakes
and the snails are six instead
of three feet under

i quilted myself
one blanket and purchased five
pounds of colored popcorn
in corners i placed dried
flowers and in my bathroom a jar
of lavendar smells
my landlord stripped my windows
and i cut all my old sox for feet pads

they say you should fight the cold with the cold
but since i never do anything right
i called you

RAIN

rain is
god's sperm falling
in the receptive
woman how else
to spend
a rainy day
other than with you
seeking sun and stars
and heavenly bodies
how else to spend
a rainy day
other than with you

POETRY IS A TRESSEL

poetry is a tressel
spanning the distance between
what i feel
and what i say

like a locomotive
i rush full speed ahead
trusting your strength
to carry me over

sometimes we share a poem
because people are near
and they would notice me
noticing you
so i write X and you write O
and we both win

sometimes we share a poem
because i'm washing the dishes
and you're looking at your news

or sometimes we make a poem
because it's Sunday and you want
ice cream while i want cookies

but always we share a poem
because belief predates action
and i believe
the most beautiful poem
ever heard is your heart
racing

THE LAWS OF MOTION

(for Harlem Magic)

The laws of science teach us a pound of gold weighs as much as a pound of flour though if dropped from any undetermined height in their natural state one would reach bottom and one would fly away

Laws of motion tell us an inert object is more difficult to propel than an object heading in the wrong direction is to turn around. Motion being energy—inertia—apathy. Apathy equals hostility. Hostility—violence. Violence being energy is its own virtue. Laws of motion teach us

Black people are no less confused because of our Blackness than we are diffused because of our powerlessness. Man we are told is the only animal who smiles with his lips. The eyes however are the mirror of the soul

The problem with love is not what we feel but what we wish we felt when we began to feel we should feel something. Just as publicity is not production: seduction is not seductive

If I could make a wish I'd wish for all the knowledge of all the world. Black may be beautiful Professor Micheau says but knowledge is power. Any desirable object is bought and sold—any neglected object declines in value. It is against man's nature to be in either category

If white defines Black and good defines evil then men define women or women scientifically speaking describe men. If sweet is the opposite of sour and heat the absence of cold then love is the contradiction of pain and beauty is in the eye of the beheld

Sometimes I want to touch you and be touched in return. But you think I'm grabbing and I think you're shirking and Mama always said to look out for men like you

So I go to the streets with my lips painted red and my eyes carefully shielded to seduce the world my reluctant lover

And you go to your men slapping fives feeling good posing as a man because you know as long as you sit very very still the laws of motion will be in effect

ALONE

i can be
alone by myself
i was
lonely alone
now i'm lonely
with you
something is wrong
there are flies
everywhere
i go

HOW DO YOU WRITE A POEM?

how do you write a poem
about someone so close
to you that when you say ahhhhh
they say chuuuu
what can they ask you to put
on paper that isn't already written
on your face
and does the paper make it
any more real
that without them
life would be not
impossible but certainly
more difficult
and why would someone need
a poem to say when i come
home if you're not there
i search the air
for your scent
would i search any less
if i told the world
i don't care at all
and love is so complete
that touch or not we blend
to each other the things
that matter aren't all about
baaaanging (i can be baaaanged all
day long) but finding a spot

where i can be free
of all the physical
and emotional demands
and simply sit with a cup
of coffee and say to you
"i'm tired" don't you know
those are my love words
and say to you "how was your
day" doesn't that show
i care or say to you "we lost
a friend" and not want to share
that loss with strangers
don't you already know
what i feel and if
you don't maybe
i should check my feelings

SOMETHING TO BE
SAID FOR SILENCE

there is something
to be said for silence
    it's almost as sexual as moving
    your bowels

i wanted to be in love
when winter came
like a groundhog i would burrow
under the patchwork pieces
of your love
but the threads are slender
and they are being stretched

i guess it's all right
to want to feel
though it's better to really feel
and sometimes i wonder
did i ever love anyone

i like my house my job i gave up
my car
but i bought a new coat
and somewhere something is missing
    i do all the right things
maybe i'm just tired
maybe i'm just tired of being tired
i feel sometimes so inert
and laws of motion being what they are
i feel we won't feel again

it's all right with me
if you want to love
it's all right with me if you don't
my silence is at least
as sexy as your love
and twice as easy
to take

THE LION IN DANIEL'S DEN

(for Paul Robeson, Sr.)

on the road to damascus
to slay the christians
saul saw the light
and was blinded by that light
and looked into the Darkness
and embraced that Darkness
and saul arose from the great white way
saying "I Am Paul
who would slay you
but I saw the Darkness
and I am that Darkness"
then he raised his voice
singing red black and green songs
saying "I am the lion
in daniel's den
I am the lion thrown to slaughter"

do not fear the lion
for he is us
and we are all
in daniel's den

III. And Some Places

AFRICA

i am a teller of tales
a dreamer of dreams
    shall i spin a poem around you
human beings grope to strangers
to share a smile
complain to lovers of their woes
and never touch
those who need to be touched
    may i move on
the african isn't independent
he's emancipated
and like the freedman he explores
his freedom rather than exploits
his nation
worrying more about the condition
of the women than his position in the world
    i am a dreamer of dreams
in my fantasy i see a person
not proud for pride is a collection of lions
or a magazine in washington d.c.
but a person who can be wrong and go on
or a person who can be praised and still work
but a person who can let a friend share a joy as easily
as a friend shares a sorrow
it's odd that all welcome a tale of disappointment
though few a note of satisfaction
have none of us been happy
    i am a teller of tales
i see kings and noblemen
slaves and serfs all selling
and being sold for what end
to die for freedom or live for joy
    i am a teller of tales

we must believe in each other's dreams
i'm told and i dream
of me accepting you and you accepting yourself
will that stroke the tension
between blacks and africans
i dream of truth lubricating our words
will that ease three hundred years
and i dream of black men and women walking
together side by side into a new world
described by love and bounded by difference
for nothing is the same except oppression and shame
     may i spin a poem around you
come let's step into my web
and dream of freedom together

SWAZILAND

i am old and need
to remember
you are young and need
to learn
if i forget the words
will you remember the music

i hear a drum speaking of a stream
the path is crossing the stream
the stream is crossing the path
which came first the drums ask
the music is with the river

if we meet does it matter
that i took the step toward you

the words ask are you fertile
the music says let's dance

i am old and need to remember
you are young and want to learn
let's dance together
let's dance
together
let's
dance
together

A VERY SIMPLE WISH

i want to write an image
like a log-cabin quilt pattern
and stretch it across all the lonely
people who just don't fit in
    we might make a world
    if i do that

i want to boil a stew
with all the leftover folk
whose bodies are full
of empty lives
    we might feed a world
    if i do that

twice in our lives
we need direction
when we are young and innocent
when we are old and cynical
but since the old refused
to descipline us
we now refuse
to discipline them
which is a contemptuous way
for us to respond
to each other

i'm always surprised
that it's easier to stick
a gun in someone's face
or a knife in someone's back
than to touch skin to skin
anyone whom we like

i should imagine if nature holds true
one day we will lose our hands

since we do no work nor make
any love
if nature is true
we shall all lose our eyes
since we cannot even now distinguish
the good from the evil

i should imagine we shall lose our souls
since we have so blatantly put them up
for sale and glutted the marketplace
thereby depressing the price

i wonder why we don't love
not some people way on
the other side of the world with strange
customs and habits
not some folk from whom we were sold
hundreds of years ago
but people who look like us
who think like us
who want to love us   why
don't we love them

i want to make a quilt
of all the patches and find
one long strong pole
to lift it up

i've a mind to build
a new world

want to play

WALKING DOWN PARK

walking down park
amsterdam
or columbus do you ever stop
to think what it looked like
before it was an avenue
did you ever stop to think
what you walked
before you rode
subways to the stock
exchange (we can't be on
the stock exchange
we are the stock
exchanged)

did you ever maybe wonder
what grass was like before
they rolled it
into a ball and called
it central park
where syphilitic dogs
and their two-legged tubercular
masters fertilize
the corners and sidewalks
ever want to know what would happen
if your life could be fertilized
by a love thought
from a loved one
who loves you

ever look south
on a clear day and not see
time's squares but see
tall birch trees with sycamores
touching hands
and see gazelles running playfully
after the lions

ever hear the antelope bark
from the third floor apartment

ever, did you ever, sit down
and wonder about what freedom's freedom
would bring
it's so easy to be free
you start by loving yourself
then those who look like you
all else will come
naturally

ever wonder why
so much asphalt was laid
in so little space
probably so we would forget
the Iroquois, Algonquin
and Mohicans who could caress
the earth

ever think what Harlem would be
like if our herbs and roots and elephant ears
grew sending
a cacophony of sound to us
the parrot parroting black is beautiful black is beautiful
owls sending out whooooo's making love . . .
and me and you just sitting in the sun trying
to find a way to get a banana from one of the monkeys
koala bears in the trees laughing at our listlessness

ever think it's possible
for us to be
happy

NIGHT

in africa night walks
into day as quickly
as a moth is extinguished
by its desire for flame

the clouds in the caribbean carry
night like a young man
with a proud erection dripping
black dots across the blue sky
the wind a mistress of the sun howls
her displeasure at the involuntary
fertilization

but nights are white
in new york
the shrouds of displeasure
mask our fear of facing
ourselves between the lonely
sheets

NO RESERVATIONS
(for Art Jones)

there are no reservations
for the revolution

no polite little clerk
to send notice
to your room
saying you are WANTED
on the battlefield

there are no banners
to wave you forward
no blaring trumpets
not even a blues note
moaning wailing lone blue note
to the yoruba drums saying
strike now   shoot
strike now   fire
strike now   run

there will be no grand
parade
and a lot thrown round
your neck
people won't look up and say
"why he used to live next to me
isn't it nice
it's his turn now"

there will be no recruitment
station
where you can give
the most convenient hours
"monday wednesday i play ball
friday night i play cards
any other time i'm free"

there will be no reserve
of energy
no slacking off till next time
"let's see—i can come back
next week
better not wear myself out
this time"

there will be reservations
only
if we fail

SOMETIMES

sometimes
when i wake up
in the morning
and see all the faces
i just can't
breathe

ALABAMA POEM

if trees could talk
    wonder what they'd say
met an old man
    on the road late afternoon
    hat pulled over to shade
    his eyes
    jacket slumped over his
    shoulders
    told me "girl! my hands seen
    more than all
    them books they got
    at tuskegee"
    smiled at me
    half waved his hand
    walked on down the dusty road
met an old woman
    with a corncob pipe
    sitting and rocking
    on a spring evening
    "sista" she called to me
    "let me tell you—my feet
    seen more than yo eyes
    ever gonna read"
    smiled at her and kept
    on moving
    gave it a thought and went
    back to the porch
    "i say gal" she called down

"you a student at the institute?
better come here and study
these feet
i'm gonna cut a bunion off
soons i gets up"
i looked at her
she laughed at me
if trees would talk
wonder what they'd tell me

POETRY

poetry is motion graceful
as a fawn
gentle as a teardrop
strong like the eye
finding peace in a crowded room

we poets tend to think
our words are golden
though emotion speaks too
loudly to be defined
by silence

sometimes after midnight or just before
the dawn
we sit typewriter in hand
pulling loneliness around us
forgetting our lovers or children
who are sleeping
ignoring the weary wariness
of our own logic
to compose a poem
     no one understands it
it never says "love me" for poets are
beyond love
it never says "accept me" for poems seek not
acceptance but controversy
it only says "i am" and therefore
i concede that you are too

a poem is pure energy
horizontally contained
between the mind
of the poet and the ear of the reader
if it does not sing discard the ear
for poetry is song
if it does not delight discard
the heart for poetry is joy
if it does not inform then close
off the brain for it is dead
if it cannot heed the insistent message
that life is precious

which is all we poets
wrapped in our loneliness
are trying to say

ALWAYS THERE ARE
THE CHILDREN

and always   there are the children

there will be children in the heat of day
there will be children in the cold of winter

children   like a quilted blanket
are welcomed in our old age

children   like a block of ice to a desert sheik
are a sign of status in our youth

we feed the children with our culture
that they might understand our travail

we nourish the children on our gods
that they may understand respect

we urge the children on the tracks
that our race will not fall short

but children are not ours
nor we theirs   they are future   we are past

how do we welcome the future
not with the colonialism of the past
    for that is our problem
not with the racism of the past
    for that is their problem
not with the fears of our own status
    for history is lived not dictated

we welcome the young of all groups
as our own with the solid nourishment
of food and warmth

we prepare the way with the solid
nourishment of self-actualization

we implore all the young to prepare for the young
because always there will be children

Rome 12 November 1974